D0121484

Israel and the Arab Nations in Conflict

NATHANIEL HARRIS

WAYLAND

First published in 1998 by
Wayland Publishers Ltd,
61 Western Road,
Hove,
East Sussex BN3 1JD

This book was prepared for Wayland Publishers Ltd
by Ruth Nason.

Series editor: Alex Woolf
Series design: Stonecastle Graphics
Book design: LNbooks, Houghton Regis, Bedfordshire

Find Wayland on the internet at:
http://www.wayland.co.uk

British Library Cataloguing in Publication Data
Harris, Nathaniel, 1937-
  Israel and the Arab Nations in conflict. – (New perspectives)
  1.Israel-Arab conflicts - Juvenile literature
  I.Title
  956'.04

ISBN 0 7502 2169 0

Printed and bound in Italy by G. Canale & C.S.p.A., Turin

Cover photos: Israeli tanks
on a training exercise in
the Golan Heights, 1991;
an Arab opponent of the
peace talks, 1991.

Page 1: Israeli vehicles push
into the Sinai Peninsula.
This mainly desert Egyptian
territory was overrun by
Israel in 1956 and 1967.

Acknowledgements

The Author and Publishers thank the following for their permission
to reproduce photographs: Camera Press: pages 1, 3, 9, 15, 16, 19t,
22t, 26, 27t, 29, 30, 32, 36, 38, 39, 40, 42, 43, 44, 45, 48, 49, 50b, 51,
54; Getty Images: pages 13, 17, 19b, 21, 22b, 25, 34, 35; John Frost
Historical Newspaper Service: page 33; Mary Evans Picture Library:
pages 12, 14; Popperfoto: pages 4, 6, 7, 18, 23t, 24, 27b, 31, 37, 46,
47, 55, 56, 57, 59; Rex Features Ltd: pages 5 (Heidi Levine/Sipa
Press), 52 (Yoav Lemmer/Sipa Press); TRIP/A. Farago: page 10;
Topham Picturepoint: cover and pages 23b, 50t, 53.

CONTENTS

1996: Israeli soldiers in Hebron, a key city in peace agreements made between the Palestinian and Israeli authorities.

DEATH OF A LEADER

A killer's targets. Israeli Foreign Minister Shimon Peres (left) and Prime Minister Yitzhak Rabin wave to the crowd in the Kings of Israel Square, 4 November 1995. A few minutes later Rabin was shot by a fellow-Jew, Yigal Amir (opposite).

The peace rally was held in Tel Aviv, the largest and most modern city in Israel. The idea of this great, open-air mass meeting was to celebrate agreements that had been made between the Israeli government and the leaders of the Palestinian people. If the agreements led to a lasting peace, they would end decades of conflict, brutality and terror which had darkened the lives of the mainly Jewish Israelis and the Arab Palestinians. But the prime minister of Israel, Yitzhak Rabin, was not certain that the rally would be a success. There was a good deal of opposition to the peace programme among both Israelis and Palestinians. Furthermore the rally was to take place in the Kings of Israel Square, which could hold at least 50,000 people: would so many come, or would there be a humiliatingly low turnout?

Rabin need not have worried. On 4 November 1995, more than a quarter of a million enthusiastic Israelis were crammed into the square and the streets leading into it. The prime minister arrived at about 8 pm, went straight up on to the stage, and made a stirring speech.

He told the crowd that the peace process was the only way to make Israel secure, even though it involved giving up territory. He praised the Palestinian leaders who were working with him to carry the process forward. And he called for 'a stand against violence' in Israel itself, where political opponents were calling one another murderers and traitors, and making all sorts of wild threats. The democratic way of deciding what should be done, said Rabin, was to hold elections, not to reach for a gun.

While the crowd clapped its approval, the normally reserved Rabin embraced his foreign minister, Shimon Peres; the two men had formerly been rivals, but peacemaking had brought them together. When a singer, Miri Aloni, took centre stage to perform the well-known 'Song of Peace', Rabin and Peres stood on either side of her and sang along. Then, after a performance by Israel's pop idol, Aviv Geffen, the rally came to a triumphant end.

The assassin

Yitzhak Rabin was not killed by one of his old Palestinian enemies, but by a fellow-Jew. Yigal Amir was a law student at the Bar-Ilan University in Tel Aviv. At 25, he already had a long record of agitation against Rabin's government and the proposals for peace between the mainly Jewish state of Israel and the Palestinians.

The agreements being celebrated at the rally in 1995 involved Israel giving up control of territories which its army had occupied.
To people like Amir, this was treason. Amir, his brother and at least one other militant had shadowed Rabin for months with the idea of killing him, but in the end Amir acted alone. After his arrest, he was quite calm, asserting that:

'I did it to save the state. He who endangers the Jewish people, his end is death. He deserved to die, and I did the job for the Jewish people.'

He even claimed that the assassination was a religious duty:

'According to religious law, when a Jew gives up his land and his people to the enemy, one is obliged to kill him.'
(Quoted in Horovitz, ed., *Yitzhak Rabin: Soldier of Peace*)

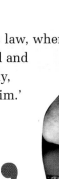

Shots in the back

Rabin and Peres left together, heading for a back staircase which led to a parking place. But when Rabin stopped to speak to the mayor of Tel Aviv, Peres went on. He passed a young man who appeared to be standing about in a relaxed fashion; everyone seems to have assumed that he was one of the drivers waiting for their employers to come down from the stage. Peres reached his car and decided not to wait for Rabin to catch up. This probably saved his life, for the relaxed young man, Yigal Amir, was an armed fanatic who intended to kill both Rabin and Peres. When he saw the two leaders separate, Amir preferred to save his bullets for the prime minister. Peres drove away without realizing that he had come very close to death.

Israeli pop star Aviv Geffen at a music awards ceremony in Jerusalem, September 1996.
A flamboyant, controversial figure, Geffen was outspoken in favour of peace between Arabs and Jews.

The eye-witness

The 24-year-old pop star Aviv Geffen, who performed his own song, 'I cry for you', at the peace rally, was an eye-witness to the shooting of Rabin.

'I saw him fall. I saw the blood and could smell the gunshot. In that moment I knew things had changed in Israel. When they started shooting in the name of God I knew Israel was not the place to be.' (Quoted in *The Observer*, 15 June 1997)

Geffen was referring to the religious motivation claimed by the assassin.

Geffen was well-known as a controversial 'protest' singer, strongly opposed to war. In 1997, following a knife attack and death threats, he left Israel and settled in London.

Soon afterwards Rabin came down the stairs, waving to a group of supporters he could see in the distance. He reached the ground and, escorted by five bodyguards, headed for the Cadillac which stood only a few steps away. The figure of Amir emerged from the shadows and somehow slipped between the prime minister and his bodyguard. Standing close behind Rabin, he fired three times. Remarkably, one shot missed and struck a bodyguard in the shoulder. But the other two entered the prime minister's back, and the wounded man fell to the floor.

Almost immediately police officers leaped upon the assassin. A bodyguard helped Rabin into his car. The driver asked the wounded man how he felt, and Rabin answered 'Not so bad', but then lost consciousness. The Cadillac raced to the nearest hospital, but two dumdum bullets had penetrated Rabin's lungs and his condition was hopeless. Within minutes of his arrival he was dead, although surgeons spent almost an hour trying desperately to revive him.

Rabin had warned against the rise of violence in a divided Israel. His murder added another twist to a long and tangled history that had its roots in the distant past.

A divided land. The 1995 peace agreements had Arab as well as Jewish enemies. Arab suicide bombing tactics took many lives. The picture shows the remains of a bus blown up in Jerusalem in August 1995.

The area coloured orange represents Palestine under British rule (1920-48), later bitterly contested between Jews and Arabs.

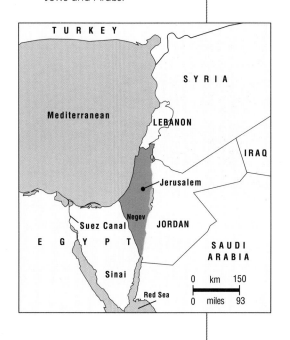

ARABS AND JEWS

The conflict described in this book has involved most countries in the Middle East. It has also had an important influence on international politics. But its centre is a relatively small area on the eastern shores of the Mediterranean, nowadays bounded by Lebanon and Syria to the north, Jordan to the east, and Egypt to the south. This area has most commonly been known as Palestine, although there has never been an independent state with that name. It is also often called the Holy Land, since it is regarded as a sacred place by followers of three great religions, Jews, Christians and Muslims.

Eye-witness: Jerusalem destroyed

Jews and Philistines, Romans, Arabs, Crusaders, Turks and British have fought over Palestine. In AD 66 the Jews rebelled against Roman rule. One of the Jewish leaders was Josephus, who eventually surrendered to the Romans. As a result he lived to witness and record the capture of Jerusalem in AD 70. At its climax:

'While the Sanctuary was burning, looting went on right and left and all who were caught were put to the sword. There was no pity for age, no regard for rank; little children and old men, laymen and priests alike were butchered; every class was held in the iron embrace of war, whether they defended themselves or cried for mercy ... The Temple Hill, enveloped in flames from top to bottom, appeared to be boiling up from its very roots; yet the sea of flame was nothing to the ocean of blood, or the companies of killers to the armies of killed: nowhere could the ground be seen between the corpses, and the soldiers climbed over heaps of bodies as they chased the fugitives.' (*The Jewish War*)

'Next year in Jerusalem'

The Jews became dispersed all round the world. But even after a thousand years or more, their original homeland was not forgotten. In fact:

'The lost Land remained central to ... Jewish law. Wherever they were, Jews turned in prayer, as they turn today, to Jerusalem ... and the words "Next year in Jerusalem", annually repeated [at Passover] by Jews throughout the world, lost none of their force or meaning.' (Samuel, *A History of Israel*)

In ancient times Palestine included territory on both sides of the river Jordan (the east bank is now part of the state of Jordan). It was the home of the Hebrews, or Jews, for whom it was 'the Promised Land' given to them by God. The Jews were unusual in believing that there was only one universal God rather than a number of different gods. Their history and their religion, Judaism, are described in the Jewish Bible.

Two small Jewish kingdoms, Israel and Judah, existed in ancient Palestine, but eventually the area was taken over by larger, stronger powers. In the late first century BC, Palestine became part of the mighty Roman Empire, which had spread all round the Mediterranean. Soon afterwards, Jesus of Nazareth was born into the Jewish community in Palestine. His teachings became the basis of Christianity, a religion that was to have a world-wide influence. However, most Jews remained faithful to Judaism. Their hatred of Rome and its gods broke out in a series of revolts which finally led to disaster. In AD 135 the Romans crushed the last Jewish resistance, and the Jewish people were driven from their capital, Jerusalem. In time they became scattered over many lands, and this dispersal, or Diaspora, became the central fact of Jewish existence for centuries to come.

Holy place: Jews pray at the Western Wall, Jerusalem, all that remains of the great temple destroyed by the Romans in AD 70.

Conquerors

After the Diaspora the history of Palestine remained troubled. It belonged to the Christianized Roman Empire until the seventh century, when it was captured by Arab forces in the name of Islam. Islam was a new religion, based on the teachings of the prophet Muhammad; its followers were known as Muslims. They regarded the Jewish prophets and Jesus as forerunners of Islam, and Jerusalem was as much a holy place for Muslims as for Jews and Christians.

Holy place: Muslims pray outside the Dome of the Rock, Jerusalem, built in the 7th century AD.

The Middle East became the centre of a great Arab and Islamic civilization. Then, during the Middle Ages, came the Crusades, a series of European Christian attempts to conquer the Holy Land. They failed, and the great majority of Arabs throughout the Middle East remained Muslims; but there were also substantial Christian and Jewish minorities in a number of places. New conquerors appeared, and Arab power collapsed. From the fifteenth century the Arab peoples were the subjects of an expanding Ottoman Turkish empire. The Turks were Muslims but not Arabs. Later, Turkey became weak, and by the late nineteenth century Palestine and other Turkish provinces were backward parts of a decaying empire.

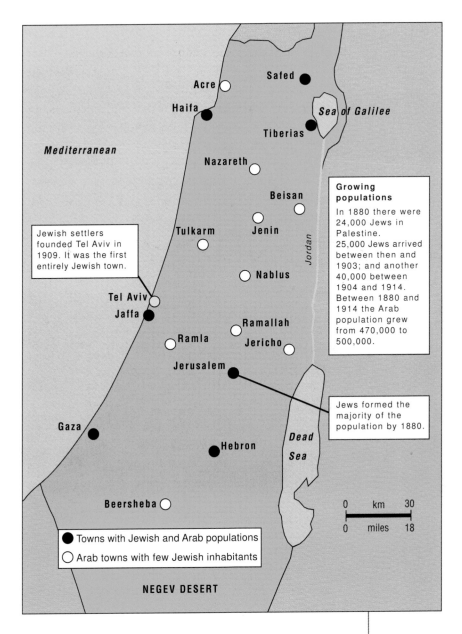

Acre

Safed

Haifa

Sea of Galilee

Tiberias

Mediterranean

Nazareth

Beisan

Growing populations

In 1880 there were 24,000 Jews in Palestine. 25,000 Jews arrived between then and 1903; and another 40,000 between 1904 and 1914. Between 1880 and 1914 the Arab population grew from 470,000 to 500,000.

Jewish settlers founded Tel Aviv in 1909. It was the first entirely Jewish town.

Tulkarm

Jenin

Jordan

Nablus

Tel Aviv

Jaffa

Ramallah

Ramla

Jericho

Jerusalem

Jews formed the majority of the population by 1880.

Gaza

Dead Sea

Hebron

Beersheba

0 km 30

0 miles 18

● Towns with Jewish and Arab populations

○ Arab towns with few Jewish inhabitants

NEGEV DESERT

Anti-Semitism

Meanwhile the Jews had suffered centuries of persecution in many lands; such persecution is known as anti-Semitism. Though robbed and sometimes massacred, herded into ghettos (separate living areas) or driven from place to place, the Jews remained a distinct religious community. Regarded in most countries as 'foreigners', they remained deeply attached to the distant Holy Land.

The main towns in Palestine, in the early 20th century. Many of the Jews who came to Palestine between 1880 and 1914 set up new settlements throughout the country.

During the nineteenth century, conditions improved dramatically for Jews in Europe, and many began to be accepted, and to behave, as ordinary, loyal citizens of the states in which they lived. But violent attacks on Jewish communities flared up in backward Russia, and there was still much prejudice elsewhere, even towards secular (non-religious) Jews. One of these, Theodor Herzl (1860-1904), became convinced that the only solution was for the Jewish people to stop being a persecuted minority and have a country of their own.

Anti-Semitism: the problem

Theodor Herzl (1860-1904) was an Austrian Jewish journalist and lawyer. Seeing that Jews were persecuted in civilized France as well as backward Russia, he came to believe that they would never be left in peace while they lived among other peoples:

'In vain are we loyal patriots ... In vain do we make the same sacrifices of life and property as our fellow-citizens; in vain do we strive to increase the fame of our native land in science and art ... In countries where we have lived for centuries we are still cried down as strangers ... Wherever they [the Jews] live in perceptible numbers, they are more or less persecuted ...'
(From *The Jewish State*, 1896, quoted in Laqueur, *The Arab-Israeli Reader*)

FROM THE NILE TO THE NEVA.

Crime and punishment. In this cartoon from the humorous magazine *Punch* (August 1890), Russia's ruler is warned by the ghost of the Egyptian pharaoh, who perished in Biblical times through persecuting the Jews: 'That weapon always wounds the hand that wields it.'

The Zionist Dream

Herzl's idea became known as Zionism. The word comes from Zion, a hill in the heart of Jerusalem. As the name of the movement suggested, there was no real chance that Zionists would accept any land but Palestine in which to settle and, if possible, to found a new Jewish state.

The majority of Jews, though sympathetic, had no intention of leaving their homes for Palestine. But emigration did take place from the 1880s, especially from Eastern Europe where anti-Semitism was still very strong. In 1896 Herzl made his ideas better known by organizing the first international congress of Zionists at Basel in Switzerland.

To the Promised Land: East European Jews walking to Palestine in the 1930s.

 Anti-Semitism: the remedy?

Herzl argued that there was only one way to end the age-old persecution of the Jews:

'Let the sovereignty be granted us over a portion of the globe large enough to satisfy the requirements of a nation; the rest we shall manage for ourselves.' (From *The Jewish State*, 1896, quoted in Laqueur, *The Arab-Israeli Reader*)

Back to the land

In Europe, Jews had rarely been allowed to work on the land. Many of the early Jewish settlers in Palestine formed communities where manual work was done by everyone. Many joined kibbutzim, idealistic farming communities where all were equal, everything was shared out and everybody took part in decision-making.

As a young man, David Ben-Gurion, one of the founders of Israel (prime minister 1948-53, 1955-63), settled in Turkish-ruled Palestine. He recalled the pioneer atmosphere:

'I labored in grove and vineyard and wine press, later joining the farming settlement of Sejera in Galilee. There I followed the plow, and as the black clods of earth turned and crumbled, and the oxen trod with the slow and heedless dignity of their kind, I saw visions and dreamed dreams.' (*Israel: Years of Challenge*)

The new life: Zionist settlers in the north of Palestine, 1900.

There had always been some Jews in Palestine. By the late nineteenth century they formed only a small percentage of the population, although they were a majority in Jerusalem itself. The Zionists who arrived in Palestine at this time were unlike the older Jewish population: they were Europeans in outlook and appearance. Perhaps this was why Palestinian Arabs resented them, even though the Zionists bought land from them to form and cultivate their own settlements. As early as the 1880s there were Arab attacks on such settlements. Immigration remained small in scale, and while the Turks ruled Palestine the future of Zionism was uncertain.

The First World War

The First World War (1914-18) changed the world, including the Middle East. Britain, France and their allies waged war on Germany, Austria-Hungary and Turkey. Britain and France encouraged the Arabs to revolt against Turkish rule, on the understanding that independent Arab states would be established at the end of the war. In spite of this, Britain and France also intended to acquire territories for themselves from the Turkish empire. And Britain's foreign minister, Arthur Balfour, also made promises to the Jews. The Balfour Declaration of November 1917 stated that Britain would 'view with favour the establishment in Palestine of a national home for the Jewish people'.

Arthur James Balfour.

 ## The Balfour Declaration

Arthur James Balfour (1848-1930) was the British foreign minister during the First World War. The Balfour Declaration was contained in a letter dated 2 November 1917 to Lord Rothschild, a prominent British Jew. Balfour wrote that the cabinet had told him to pass on the fact that:

'His Majesty's Government view with favour the establishment in Palestine of a National Home for the Jewish people, and will use their best endeavours to facilitate the achievement of this object, it being clearly understood that nothing shall be done which may prejudice the civil and religious rights of existing non-Jewish communities in Palestine, or the rights and political status enjoyed by Jews in any other country.'

At the end of the war, the Turkish empire collapsed. In its place a number of Arab states were set up, although for a long time they were strongly influenced by Britain and France. Some arrangements were made by a new international authority, the League of Nations (which eventually became the United Nations). The League gave Palestine to Britain as a 'mandated territory' – that is, Britain was to rule the area in order to create the promised Jewish 'National Home' and prepare the country for self-government.

Palestine under British rule

In 1920, even before British rule was firmly in place, there was a series of savage Arab attacks on Jews in their settlements and in Jerusalem. Riots and disturbances took place the following year. After a peaceful interval they flared up again in 1929, and between 1936 and 1939 there was constant trouble, in the form of riots, strikes and armed attacks. The Jews organized their own self-defence force, the Haganah, but some Jewish groups, such as the Irgun Zvai Leumi, broke away from it to act more aggressively. Harsh deeds were done by both Arabs and Jews, and also by the British security forces.

British riot police go into action against Arab demonstrators, Jaffa, October 1933.

Meanwhile Jews continued to come from other lands to settle in Palestine. Their numbers were swelled in the 1930s by German Jews fleeing from persecution by the Nazis, who had taken power in 1933. There are no really reliable statistics, but by 1939 there were believed to be some 450,000 Jews in Palestine, about a third of the total population. Bearing European skills and technology, Jewish settlers made economic advances that attracted many Arab immigrants from outside Palestine. This later served to complicate discussions about the number of people who were or were not 'genuine' Palestinians.

Caught up in a conflict with no easy solution, the British found it hard to follow a consistent policy and became unpopular with both sides. In 1937 the government-appointed Peel Commission recommended that Palestine should be partitioned – divided into a Jewish and an Arab state, with Jerusalem and the area around it remaining under British rule. Jewish representatives reluctantly agreed, but the Arabs rejected the idea and the violence went on. Later talks made little progress.

Then in 1939 there was a dramatic shift in British policy: Jewish immigration was to be drastically limited and then ended altogether, and within ten years an Arab-majority Palestinian state would be set up. But the British White Paper (policy document) was rejected not only by the Jews but also by the Arabs. The Arabs wanted immediate independence and made it clear that, when they achieved it, they would force most of the Jews out of Palestine.

The Second World War

The Second World War (1939-45) had important effects on the situation. In the 1930s the Nazi regime in Germany had persecuted Jews. During the war, at a time when Germany had conquered most of Europe, the Nazis launched a programme designed to exterminate all Jews within their reach. Millions were shot, worked to death or gassed. Of the survivors, many were 'Displaced Persons', without homes or countries. They were happy to leave the places where they had suffered, and settle in a new land.

Britain kept to its policy of restricted immigration. But the sight of boatloads of Nazi victims being turned back intensified world sympathy for the Jewish people. Immigrants were smuggled in, Jewish opposition to the British hardened, and extremist Jewish groups began a terrorist campaign against them.

Partition

By February 1947 the British had had enough. They handed the problem over to the United Nations (UN), which had succeeded the League of Nations. Despite Arab opposition, the UN backed the partition of Palestine and in November 1947 a majority of its member-states approved.

Victims of war seeking a new start: Jewish immigrants arrive at Haifa, July 1946.

The United Nations plan to partition Palestine, 1947.

Haifa

Mediterranean

Jericho
Jerusalem
Gaza

Beersheba

NEGEV DESERT

To be under Jewish sovereignty
To be under Arab sovereignty
To be under international control

0   km   50
0   miles   31

In the months before the British left, Jews and Arabs began to fight for control of towns and settlements. Many thousands of Arabs fled or were driven out.

March 1948: a member of the Haganah (Jewish army) on guard in Tel Aviv during the months of violence before the British left Palestine.

66   Massacre

On 10 April 1948 Jacques de Reynier, head of the Red Cross delegation in Palestine, arrived at the village of Deir Yassin. It had been captured by a detachment of the Irgun Zvai Leumi, who had been 'cleaning up'. When de Reynier went into a house:

'I found some bodies cold. Here the "cleaning up" had been done with machine-guns, then hand-grenades. It had been finished off with knives, anyone could see that.' (Quoted in Dimbleby, *The Palestinians*)

Many other revolting details were recorded by de Reynier and by the British authorities, who would soon leave Palestine. 254 men, women and children were said to have been slaughtered at Deir Yassin. The massacre, condemned by the Jewish leadership, was reckoned the worst Jewish atrocity of the 1948-9 war. It was answered shortly afterwards by an equally horrible massacre of Jewish medical workers. **99**

On 14 May 1948 the last British High Commissioner left Palestine. The new state of Israel was proclaimed in Tel Aviv, and the armies of the neighbouring Arab countries invaded, with the openly declared aim of destroying it.

WARS, HOT AND COLD

The first Arab-Israeli war

In May 1948 the armies of Egypt, Jordan, Iraq, Syria and Lebanon all joined in an attack on the new state of Israel. They expected their troops to win a rapid victory and declared that they would 'drive the Jews into the sea'. Instead, the war lasted for over a year, during which the Israelis defended themselves successfully and then went on the offensive. When the fighting ended, Israel had gained a considerable amount of territory and the Arab states had sustained a humiliating defeat.

Israel survived, but gained only a temporary security. The fighting had ended with a series of truces between Israel and each of its enemies – but no peace treaties were signed.

Jews celebrate the founding of Israel, 14 May 1948.

11 June 1948: a street in Tel Aviv, bombed by the Egyptian air force.

Divided Palestine. The 1948-9 war gave Israel more territory than the UN partition plan shown as a map on page 17.

The Arab states remained technically at war with Israel, refused to accept its right to exist, and clearly intended to destroy it if they could.

When they were not at war with Israel, they tried to cripple it by boycotts and blockades. Israeli ships were not allowed to pass through the Egyptian-controlled Suez Canal or the Straits of Tiran, although these were international waterways that should have been open to all nations. Arab states refused to do business with any firm that had dealings with the Israelis. They even refused to allow in tourists whose passports showed that they had visited Israel.

In this situation, which lasted for almost thirty years, there could be no peace talks. Faced with relentless hostility from its neighbours, Israel became a state permanently under siege. Every Israeli was expected to serve for a time in the armed forces, and an unhealthily large proportion of the nation's resources were spent on creating and maintaining a powerful war machine.

The Arab refugees

Many thousands of Arabs fled from Jewish-controlled territory in 1948-9. Israelis and Arabs have argued about this ever since. Did they choose to go? Were they driven out? Or did they flee in panic? Whatever the truth, the result was the setting up of refugee camps around Israel's borders. Many Palestinians would spend decades in them:

'The tents of the refugees gave way gradually to concrete walls and corrugated roofs, squashed up against each other, rising in disorderly fashion, a storey added here and there ... The camps became villages, the villages grew into towns, their populations permanent but unsettled – yet remaining in ... abject misery.' (Dimbleby, *The Palestinians*)

A balanced view?

A leading Israeli historian, J.L.Talmon, described himself as 'passionately convinced of the rightness of the Jewish cause' but admitted that 'Arab rights and claims' mattered. He saw the conflict as:

'a clash of rights, for which a solution could only be found on the lines of least injustice, and where no perfect justice was possible'.
(Quoted in Laqueur, *The Arab-Israeli Reader*)

Refugees

The principal victims of the first Arab-Israeli war were the several hundred thousand Arabs who had fled or been driven from their homes in Israeli-controlled areas. Many crossed the northern border into Lebanon, while others took refuge in the parts of Palestine held by the Egyptian and Jordanian armies. These areas did not become a separate state, but were annexed by the occupying Arab powers: Egypt took the Gaza Strip, while east Jerusalem and the area on the west bank of the river Jordan became part of the kingdom of Jordan. But the displaced Palestinians did not become citizens of Egypt or Lebanon, which were unwilling to absorb them. Consequently they remained refugees, confined to camps close to the Israeli border. They lived in makeshift housing, on rations issued by the United Nations, and still dreamed of going back to their former homes. (Jordan was the exception in giving citizenship to Palestinians.)

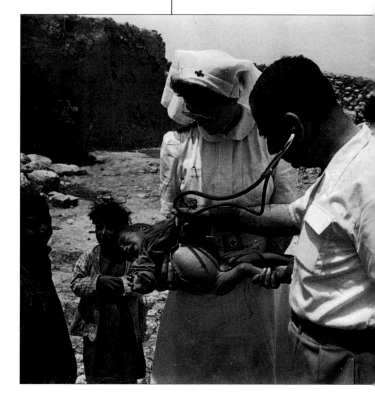

June 1949: a Red Cross doctor examines a baby at an Arab refugee camp. Immediately after the war conditions at the camps were often appalling.

David Ben-Gurion, prime minister of Israel, 1948-53 and 1955-63.

Different faces of Israel. Right: most immigrants, including adults, needed to learn the modernized form of the Hebrew language, previously known only from ancient religious texts.

Page 23 (top): a Yemenite mother and child at an Israeli refugee camp. Thrown out of Arab states, such Arabic-speaking Jews became an important element in the population.

Page 23 (bottom): Israeli troops in training. Every Israeli was required to serve for a time in the armed forces.

Developments in Israel

Meanwhile Israel was organized as a modern democracy. All citizens had equal rights and could vote in elections for one of several political parties. Moreover, the citizens included the large minority of Arabs who had not fled from the country in 1948-9. Israel's democracy impressed outsiders, especially when it was compared with the monarchies and one-party states of the Arab world.

However, Israel was clearly intended to be a mainly Jewish state. Immigration was encouraged by the Law of the Return (1950), which gave every Jew in the world the right to enter Israel and take up citizenship. Many Jews arrived from war-shattered Europe, but relatively few were prepared to leave countries such as the USA and Britain, where they were fully accepted.

The population of Israel was dramatically increased in the 1950s by the arrival of several hundred thousand

Jews who had been driven from the Arab countries in which they had lived for centuries. These 'Oriental' or Sephardic Jews were in many respects like the Arabs who had been their neighbours, and less like the Israelis of European origin (Ashkenazim) who had made Israel into a modern state. The two groups managed to live together, though not without tensions and resentments.

Terrorism and military response

Unable to defeat Israel in battle, Egypt and Jordan found other means to keep up the pressure on their foe. They trained Palestinian militants, who became known as fedayeen ('self-sacrificers'), to launch raids across their borders, killing and spreading terror before withdrawing. As a result, Israelis could never feel safe and the Israeli army acquired the habit of counter-striking into enemy territory. This pattern of terrorism and military response would be seen again and again.

The war of 1956

Changes in the Middle East raised the political temperature higher still. In 1952 an army coup overthrew the Egyptian monarchy, and soon Gamal Abdel Nasser emerged as the country's new leader. Aiming to unite and lead the Arab world, Nasser intensified the campaign against Israel. He also wanted to end the remaining influence of Britain and France in the Middle East, and in June 1956 he took over the mainly Anglo-French-owned Suez Canal, which ran through Egyptian territory. Despite British and French anger, Nasser seemed to have got his way. He went on to threaten Israel, massing troops on the frontier and forging links with Jordan and Syria.

Feeling that they could not afford to wait and see whether Nasser was bluffing, the Israelis decided to strike first. On 29 October 1956, they launched a sudden, devastating attack against Egypt, and their forces were soon driving deep into the Sinai Peninsula towards the Suez Canal.

Arab unity

Gamal Abdel Nasser (1918-70) enjoyed enormous popularity in the Arab world. In 1954 he became the head of the military regime in Egypt and hoped to unite the entire 'Arab nation'.

The link between Arab unity and hostility towards the common enemy, Israel, is clear in Nasser's speech to trade unionists just before the disastrous 1967 war:

'We are confident that once we have entered the battle we will triumph ... We [Egypt and Syria] will operate as one army fighting a single battle for the sake of a common objective – the objective of the Arab nation ... The battle will be a general one and our basic objective will be to destroy Israel.' (Quoted in Laqueur, *The Arab-Israeli Reader*)

Unknown to the world, Britain and France had made a secret agreement to help Israel and revenge themselves on Nasser. So after the outbreak of war, Anglo-French forces bombed Egyptian positions and seized the Suez Canal, claiming that they were only protecting this vital waterway. In fact, they were too late to stop the Egyptians sinking ships and blocking the Canal. The two superpowers, the USA and the Soviet Union, condemned the Anglo-French action and forced them to make a humiliating evacuation of the Canal.

The Israelis withdrew from Sinai in 1957, having gained only the suspension of terrorist attacks and an easing of the naval blockades. For Nasser, the military defeat turned into a political victory over 'imperialism', the 'empire-building', Arab-dominating policies that Britain and France still supposedly followed.

A salvage vessel (right) clears sunken shipping from the Suez Canal.

Suez: an Egyptian woman made homeless by fighting.

The Cold War

Over the next few years there were a number of upheavals in the Middle East. The Arab states often quarrelled among themselves, but their attitude towards Israel remained unchanged. The situation was complicated by the Cold War, the intense hostility (falling short of a 'hot', shooting war) between two great international alliances. One was American-led, while the other was headed by the Soviet Union (present-day Russia and most of its neighbours, which at that time formed a single country). Both alliances tried to win friends in the Middle East. Generally, the Soviets backed the Arab states and the Americans supported Israel. This made any Arab-Israeli agreement even less likely, and it also meant that both sides were generously supplied with arms and war materials – and rapidly re-supplied after any conflict.

The Six-Day War

In 1967 a new crisis began, amid rumours, threats and counter-threats. The situation became really serious when Nasser asked for the United Nations Emergency Force – in effect the force separating the Egyptians and Israelis – to withdraw from its positions. The UN left, so promptly that it was criticized for not doing enough to prevent the coming war. Removing the UN seemed to mean that Egypt was about to attack. Then the Egyptians imposed a new naval blockade of Israel's outlet on the Red Sea, while their Jordanian allies were reinforced by the arrival of Iraqi and other troops from the Arab world.

Attitudes towards the United Nations

The United Nations (UN) failed to stop the 1967 war and other Arab-Israeli conflicts. This was becaused the UN can only act effectively when its most powerful members are in agreement, or when both sides in a conflict will accept its authority. Arabs and Israelis have enthusiastically supported the UN – but only when it has suited them.

For example, in 1947-8 Arabs rejected the UN's partition plan for Palestine. Even decades later, the Palestinian leader, Yasser Arafat, declared:

'The Assembly [of the UN] partitioned what it had no right to divide – an indivisible homeland.' (Quoted in Ross, *The Arab-Israeli Conflict*)

By contrast, the Jews supported partition and condemned the Arabs for opposing the UN. Yet, according to the same UN plan, Jerusalem should have been placed under international control. The response to that of the Israeli prime minister David Ben-Gurion was:

'Jerusalem is an inseparable part of Israel and her eternal capital. No United Nations vote can alter that historic fact.' (Quoted in O'Brien, *The Siege*)

There were many further examples of this 'double standard'.

Page 26: Deadly weapon: in 1967 the Israelis' Mirage III planes devastated Egyptian and Syrian airfields.

Left: June 1967: an Israeli tank crew take part in the advance into Syria.

The fruits of victory

In his book *The Siege*, the Irish diplomat Conor Cruise O'Brien summed up the immediate response to Israel's 1967 victory:

' ... no present willingness on the part of the Arabs to negotiate anything at all with Israel. The first meeting of the Arab states after the war – the Khartoum Conference, August 19 to September 1, 1967 – issued its famous "three noes": no peace with Israel; no recognition of Israel; no negotiations with Israel regarding any Palestinian territory.'

Once again the Israelis struck first. On 5 June 1967 their planes launched a sudden attack which wiped out the air power of Egypt, Jordan and Syria. Many enemy planes were destroyed on the ground, before their pilots had time to take off. In the six days of fighting that followed, Israeli forces drove the Egyptians from Sinai, captured the old city of Jerusalem and the other Jordanian-held territories on the west bank of the river, and stormed the Golan Heights from which the Syrians had for years shelled Israeli settlements.

The spectacular 'Six Day War' brought Israel victory; but peace and security remained as far away as ever.

June 1967: Arabs flee from the West Bank.

THE PALESTINIAN RESPONSE

Fruits of victory: during the 1967 war Israel conquered vast territories, including Egypt's Sinai Peninsula and the Golan Heights in Syria. In the long run, these were likely to be traded for peace agreements; the fate of the West Bank and the Gaza Strip was less certain.

After the Six-Day War, Israel controlled all of Palestine, as well as some Egyptian and Syrian territory. A United Nations resolution called on the Israelis to give back the conquered land, but it also called for an end to the state of war and full recognition of all the states in the area (which would have included Israel). The Arab states would not recognize or make peace with Israel, so there was no chance of the resolution being obeyed.

For the time being Israel did not annex its main Palestinian conquests, the West Bank and the Gaza Strip. The Israelis described them as 'the Administered Territories', but outside Israel they were more commonly known as 'the Occupied Territories'.

By contrast, Israel did annex newly conquered East Jerusalem, so that the entire city was now part of – and the capital of – the Israeli state. The city's spiritual and historical significance for Jews made it unlikely that Israel would ever willingly give up Jerusalem, even to an international body. If peace-making ever got under way, this would be a great obstacle. But in 1967 peace was far away and there were many more immediate problems.

The Palestinians

The Israelis' victories made them the rulers of Arab populations on the West Bank and in the Gaza Strip.

Collecting water in the Djebalia refugee camp in the Gaza Strip, 1991.

These populations included some 120,000 of the people (or their descendants) who had fled Israeli-controlled areas in 1948-9. Many of them still lived in camps, in effect as refugees.

Jerusalem, 1991: Israeli soldiers patrol the city wall overlooking the Arab Market.

There were many more Palestinian Arabs in the Arab states. While some of these Palestinians found work or made careers for themselves in the Arab world or beyond, large numbers also still lived in camps, in very bad conditions.

Gradually these Palestinian Arabs developed a powerful sense of nationhood. Until the 1940s they had thought of themselves as Arabs, but had little feeling of belonging to a smaller, territorial nation; this made them very different from Egyptians, Syrians and other Arab peoples. Their outlook changed during their years of exile, when they found themselves unable to make new lives among their fellow Arabs in the states to which they had fled. Apart from a natural wish to return to their homes, the Palestinians felt bound together by their shared sufferings and by their experience of being treated as outsiders in other Arab lands.

What is a nation?

Most historians would say that a nation exists when a large number of people believe that they have a separate identity. But the idea of nationhood is so powerful that both Jews and Arabs tried to claim that their opponents were not 'really' nations. A pro-Zionist article in an American periodical, *Midstream*, in October 1967, argued that:

'At the end of World War I ... Palestine did not exist as a political or national entity as far as the Arabs were concerned. For them it was merely a geographical locality, the south of Syria. Whereas no one doubts the fierce authenticity of Arab nationalism, Palestinian Arab nationalism is an artificial creation with no roots before the British Mandate.' (Quoted in Laqueur, *The Arab-Israeli Reader*)

The 1968 Charter of the Palestine Liberation Organization (PLO) also argued that there could be such a thing as a 'false' or inauthentic nation:

'Claims of historical or religious ties of Jews with Palestine are incompatible with the facts of history and the true conception of what constitutes statehood. Judaism, being a religion, is not an independent nationality. Nor do Jews constitute a single nation with an identity of its own; they are citizens of the states to which they belong.'

Fedayeen in training. These Palestinians who made armed raids into Israel could be viewed either as 'terrorists' or as 'freedom fighters'.

The Palestinian sense of identity was strengthened in action: Palestinian guerrillas, or fedayeen, made many raids into Israel, initially armed and trained by Arab states. The raids were conducted by a number of groups, all anti-Israel but otherwise differing in their political views. The best-known were Fatah, led by Yasser Arafat, and the Popular Front for the Liberation of Palestine, led by George Habash.

After their catastrophic defeat in 1967, the Arab states lost a great deal of prestige. The Palestinians became still more militant and independent-minded, believing that they would have to rely on their own efforts to achieve their aims. Egypt and Syria, weakened by war and exposed to Israeli retaliation, refused to allow any more fedayeen operations. So Fatah and other groups moved their bases to Jordan and Lebanon and launched an ever-increasing number of attacks from there.

Fatah leader Yasser Arafat became chairman of the Palestine Liberation Organization (PLO) and came to be seen as the leader of the Palestinian people.

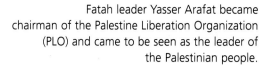

Struggle for recognition

Defeated in 1948-9, the Arab states remained hostile to Israel. They were often accused of using the Palestinians for their own political ends. And it was certainly true that for a long time Palestinian refugees were allowed little freedom by the governments that 'protected' them. Abu Jihad, one of the leaders of the Palestine Liberation Organization (PLO), described how:

'The Arabs paid lip service to our cause, but we were forbidden to organize ... So we began to realize that we should organize independently; that this was the only way to return. We were forbidden, of course, to do this openly. It was a crime to assert our Palestinian identity, even in those countries which indulged in much posturing on our behalf ... No unions – we couldn't even organize the shoemakers; no parties – political activities were forbidden to us. To say in public, "We want to return home", or, "The Arabs are the cause of our misery", was to invite the severest reprisals.' (Quoted in Dimbleby, *The Palestinians*)

Beirut, 1982: a ten-year-old PLO supporter holds up a portrait of Yasser Arafat. Despite his age, the boy has a gun and may well have had occasion to use it.

In 1968 the Palestinians won an important propaganda victory when an Israeli counter-attack into Jordan was beaten back at Karameh. The credit for this – the first success for years – went to the Fatah leader Yasser Arafat, who became a hero to many Arabs. Soon afterwards Arafat took control of the originally Egyptian-run Palestine Liberation Organization (PLO), which was joined by Fatah and the other Palestinian groups and became the main Palestinian authority.

The PLO and terrorism

Over the years, the fortunes of the PLO fluctuated. Wherever they went, the guerrillas formed a powerful armed group within the state that sheltered them.

King Hussein of Jordan, like the rulers of Egypt and Syria, did not want his country to be damaged any further by Israeli retaliation for Palestinian attacks. But a very large number of his people were Palestinians, and for a long time he found it impossible to stop PLO attacks on Israel. Eventually, in 1970-1, there was fierce fighting between royal troops and the guerrillas, ending when the PLO was driven out of the country. After this, Arafat established new bases in Lebanon, where the government was too weak and divided to prevent the Palestinians from operating as they pleased.

Meanwhile the PLO widened the scope of its activities. PLO raids into Israel had been directed mainly against civilians and civilian targets, using sub-machine guns, grenades and explosives. This kind of operation is generally described – and condemned – as terrorism, because the terrorists are not fighting an armed enemy,

Arafat the survivor

Yasser Arafat (1929-), the Palestinian leader, was the great survivor of Middle Eastern politics, holding together the PLO through many defeats. As well as opposing the Israelis, Arafat was often involved in struggles with the Arab states that were supposed to be his allies. According to Arafat himself, the Egyptians wanted to control the Palestinians, and at the beginning of the 1948 war they even disarmed them:

'I was furious. They took our weapons and we began to feel that there was something wrong. There was a betrayal ... Actually, they were not running a real war [but only] paying lip service to the idea.' (Quoted in Wallach, *Arafat: in the eyes of the beholder*)

but are trying to achieve their aims by murders that spread fear among the civilian population and make normal life impossible.

In the 1970s, Palestinian groups continued to attack Israel, but they also began to choose targets in other parts of the world. As well as direct assaults, they kidnapped people and held them as hostages, often by hijacking airliners and trains – that is, taking them over at gunpoint. The pilots of the planes were often forced to fly them to places under PLO control. In such cases, the object was usually to pressure Israel or some other country into making a concession, such as releasing PLO prisoners from its gaols.

Hostages taken by terrorists were used to blackmail governments: the *Daily Mirror*, 8 September 1970.

Among the sensational terrorist acts of the period were the blowing up of three jumbo jets (British, Swiss and American) in the Jordan desert (1970); the murder of eleven Israeli athletes at the 1972 Munich Olympics in Germany; and, in 1973, the shooting, in London, of a British businessman who raised money for Israel.

September 1970: one of the jumbo jets blown up in Jordan.

Many people were outraged by Palestinian terrorism, which took innocent lives and put everybody in danger. This was especially true in the 1970s, when other terrorist groups, such as the Italian, German and Japanese 'Red Brigades', were active in many parts of

Terrorists strike

Terrorism was a world problem in the 1970s, but Israel suffered more severely than most countries. In one such incident, members of the Democratic Front for the Liberation of Palestine seized a school building and held a hundred children as hostages. Negotiations broke down and Israeli soldiers stormed the building. According to defence minister Moshe Dayan:

'The scene was shattering, the floor covered in blood and dozens of wounded children huddled against the walls. Our soldiers had killed the three terrorists but before they were shot the assassins had managed to murder 16 of the school children and wound 68.' (*The Story of My Life*)

the world. Each group had its own objectives, but different types of terrorist groups often helped one another, and the Palestinians found powerful allies. In 1972, for example, Japanese Red Brigade members shot down twenty-five people at Tel Aviv airport; and in 1975 the pro-Palestinian Venezuelan terrorist 'Carlos' kidnapped the ministers of eleven governments at a conference in Vienna.

Palestinian terrorism angered the world and seemed obviously evil. But those who defended it argued that there was no alternative to terrorism. Because of Israel's military might, the Palestinians had no other way of fighting back. Similarly, spectacular acts of violence beyond Israel's borders were justified as the only way of making an indifferent world take notice of the Palestinians' plight.

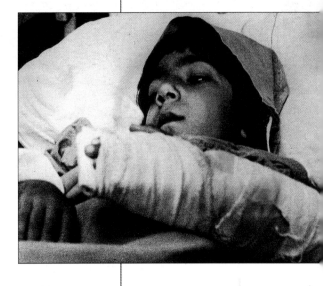

This child was injured when Arab rockets were fired from Jordan into her school playground, June 1970.

To some extent, the policy worked. In 1974 the PLO was recognized by all the Arab states as 'the sole legitimate representative of the Palestinian people'. This meant that a liberated West Bank would not return to Jordanian control, but would be run by the PLO as an independent Palestinian state. Shortly afterwards, when Arafat was invited to address the United Nations General Assembly, it became clear that the Palestinians were no longer a forgotten people.

With the Arab states and the Soviet Union and its allies on their side, the Palestinians had many friends in the UN. But whether UN resolutions could help them was another question. Meanwhile terrorism alienated the USA and European countries. And, more important in the long run, it was bound to harden Israeli attitudes towards the Palestinians. Within a few years it produced major political changes in Israel that would make a settlement harder than ever to achieve.

NO END IN SIGHT

The October War

While the PLO kept up its campaign of violence, the Arab states remained quiet for six years. Then Egypt and Syria struck against Israel on 6 October 1973. This was Yom Kippur, or the Day of Atonement, the most solemn of Jewish religious festivals. The war that followed is known as the Yom Kippur or October War.

The Israelis had been expecting an attack, but not quite so soon. Their earlier victories had made them over-confident, and they had prepared too slowly. There was dismay and confusion when the Syrians launched a ferocious assault on the Golan Heights with massed tanks, while the Egyptians crossed the Suez Canal into Sinai and began to capture the line of powerful fortresses that defended it. The impact of the attack rattled the Israelis, and they suffered heavy casualties.

Into Sinai, October 1973: an elated Egyptian soldier waves his rifle after a successful crossing of the Suez Canal.

Days of hard fighting followed, and the balance of advantage changed. The Syrians were driven back, and Israeli forces established themselves on the road to Damascus, the Syrian capital. On 15 October Israeli units crossed the Suez Canal, and within a week the Egyptian Third Army was surrounded and facing certain destruction. However, new truces ended the fighting and eventually the armies on all sides withdrew behind their borders.

The Egyptians and Syrians had suffered great losses in lives and weaponry. But Israel's much smaller losses were still heavy in proportion to its population. Israelis felt that their leaders had made a mess of things and that the state had been in great danger. Arabs, on the other hand, felt that their soldiers had fought well and had at last wiped out the shame of their 1967 defeat.

The counter-offensive: the Israeli Minister of Defence, General Moshe Dayan (left), observes his troops' advance into Syria.

On the brink

For many years the world lived in fear of a nuclear war between the USA and the Soviet Union. Clashes of interest in the Middle East were particularly threatening, but one or other of the superpowers had the sense to draw back and, if necessary, made its allies follow suit.

Late in October 1973, for example, when Israel seemed poised to destroy the Egyptian Third Army, the Soviet Union threatened to intervene. To prevent this, the US Secretary of State, Henry Kissinger, made the Israelis accept a cease-fire. When Israel's ambassador to the USA, Simcha Dinitz, tried to argue, Kissinger cut him off with a clumsy but blunt answer:

'You will be forced if it reaches that point.' (Kissinger, *Years of Upheaval*)

Israel under Begin

The long-term effects of the October War were important. Israelis blamed their government, and this was one of the reasons for the dramatic election result that occurred in May 1977. The Labour Party, which had ruled Israel ever since 1948, suffered its first defeat. A new government took over, led by Menachem Begin, chief of the Likud party and, in the struggles of the 1940s, the leader of the extreme Irgun Zvai Leumi group.

A new Jewish settlement on the West Bank, 1984.

Likud took a much more 'hard-line' attitude towards the Arabs. Begin and his followers called the Israeli-occupied West Bank 'Judea and Samaria', names used in Biblical times when the area was mainly inhabited by Jews. This was a clear signal that they regarded the West Bank as part of Israel, to be held for ever.

Although Begin did not risk annexing the Occupied Territories, he did encourage Jewish settlers to move into them. Some settlements had been established by earlier governments, mainly in areas where few Arabs lived and, it was said, mainly to strengthen Israel's defences. Under Begin, this kind of restraint no longer applied, and settlement in Arab areas was enthusiastically supported.

Jewish settlers in their West Bank home.

Israel and Egypt make peace

Begin viewed the very large Sinai Peninsula in quite a different light from the West Bank and the Gaza Strip. Sinai was Egyptian territory, held by Israel since the 1967 war, and Begin was willing to return it if Egypt would make peace.

Under Nasser's successor, Anwar Sadat, Egypt's policies were changing fast. Sadat had launched the Yom Kippur attack on Israel, but this, by restoring Arab pride, actually made it easier for him to negotiate an honourable peace. In November 1977 Sadat offered to go to Israel and speak to Israel's parliament, the Knesset. This was a bold gesture, since Arab leaders had always refused to have anything to do with Israel. Begin issued an invitation and the visit took place.

At Camp David, USA, 1978: US President Jimmy Carter smiles as Egyptian President Anwar Sadat (left) and Israeli Prime Minister Menachem Begin shake hands.

The real bargaining began after that, and proved difficult. American pressure was important in bringing about a result, and the final talks were held in the USA at Camp David, the US president's holiday home. Finally, on 26 March 1979, Sadat, Begin and US President Jimmy Carter signed a peace treaty.

Motives

It is often difficult to say why politicians act as they do. Two or more very different reasons can be put forward for many decisions. After the Camp David agreement, the Egyptian president Anwar Sadat was widely praised as a peacemaker, but the writer Conor Cruise O'Brien suggested that his motives were less noble:

'Sadat's prestige needed enhancement ... he needed to answer those Egyptians who talked of him as Nasser's unworthy successor with the words ... "Nasser lost Sinai to Israel, Sadat got it back".' (*The Siege*)

Under the Camp David agreement, the Israelis would withdraw from Sinai over a three-year period. Israel and Egypt recognized each other and arranged for normal diplomatic and trade relationships. Israeli ships could use the Suez Canal. And there would eventually be talks about some form of Palestinian self-rule on the West Bank and in the Gaza Strip, a vague provision that committed Begin to very little.

The terms of the treaty were carried out by both sides, but they did not lead to the hoped-for general peace. In fact, most other Arab states condemned Sadat as a traitor, and his making peace with Israel may have been one of the factors leading to his assassination in October 1981. After this, Egyptian-Israeli relations became less friendly, but the peace held.

1982: Israeli soldiers move into a divided Lebanon. The man offering them refreshment, a Shia Muslim, probably shared their hostility to the PLO fighters.

Into the Lebanon

Meanwhile Lebanon remained the headquarters of the PLO and also its base for direct attacks on Israel. Lebanon was a deeply divided country, beset by rivalries between the main religious groups (Maronite Christians, Sunni Muslims and Shia Muslims) as well as political conflicts. The presence of the Palestinians helped to weaken Lebanon's fragile political system, and when this collapsed in 1975 the country was plunged into a devastating civil war. Militias representing different groups fought one another and the PLO, while the Syrian army also became involved. The Lebanese capital, Beirut, formerly a prosperous modern city, was reduced to ruins.

During all this, the PLO managed to maintain a strong position, especially in the south of Lebanon. From there it could launch raids into Israel and subject northern Israeli settlements to relentless bombardments. Israel responded by helping the Maronite Lebanese, who were the PLO's enemies in the south, and by retaliatory raids after particularly successful PLO attacks. In 1978 the Israeli army invaded Lebanon to push back the PLO, withdrawing to make way for United Nations forces.

1982: Beirut under Israeli bombardment. Lebanon's civil wars ravaged this once-prosperous city.

But neither the UN intervention nor various ceasefires worked, and in 1982 a re-elected Likud government decided to act more forcefully. Earlier in the year, Israeli bombers had destroyed an Iraqi nuclear reactor, making sure that Iraq's dictator, Saddam Hussein, would not be able to develop and use nuclear weapons against Israel. The action was popular in Israel, and probably encouraged the government to intervene in the Lebanon. Operation 'Peace for Galilee' (that is, northern Israel) was launched on 6 June 1982, when Israeli army units again thrust into PLO-controlled territory.

Officially the aim of the invasion was to drive the PLO back some 40 kilometres to the north; from that distance, northern Israel would be safe from attack.

But in reality the Israelis intended to break the PLO once and for all and put in a Lebanese government that was relatively friendly to Israel. Instead of ending the offensive after a few days, the army pressed on, capturing huge quantities of weapons, until they had surrounded the PLO forces in Beirut.

This was when the difficulties started. The PLO held out for two months before accepting defeat and agreeing to leave Lebanon for Tunisia, far from the 'front line'. A new Lebanese president, Bashir Gemayal, took office; as the leader of the Maronite Falangist party, he was seen as anti-Palestinian and relatively friendly towards Israel, but he had little real power and was assassinated within a few weeks of taking office. Complicated faction-fights continued, and the Israeli army's involvement in Lebanon showed no sign of ending.

Tel Aviv, 1982: a group of Jewish Israelis demonstrate against Israel's presence in Lebanon, following the news of massacres at the Palestinian camps of Sabra and Chatila.

Israeli dissidents

Small groups of Jews within Israel took a very different view of events from all the main parties. The Jewish Israeli lawyer Felicia Langer made herself very unpopular by defending Palestinians accused of political crimes. Jewish radicals such as Roni Ben Efrat denounced the entire basis of the Israeli state:

'The young Israeli democracy was a fake based on the "disappearance" of the Palestinians ... that is how the Palestinian nakhbeh [the 1948-9 disaster] opened the door for the Israel democracy myth. A myth based on expelling a people and robbing a land.' (Quoted in di Giovanni, *Against the Stranger: lives in occupied territory*)

Then, in mid-September 1982, a Falangist militia massacred many inhabitants of two Palestinian camps in southern Lebanon, Sabra and Chatila. Israel was widely blamed for the massacre because the Israeli authorities controlled the area and had permitted their Falangist allies to enter the camps in search of Palestinian guerrillas. This was, at the very least, a badly judged decision, since the Falangists were likely to be thirsting for revenge so soon after the murder of Gemayal.

The massacres had an impact on world opinion. Rightly or wrongly, many people had sympathized with Israel, as a country struggling to survive against a league of enemy states and constant terrorist attacks. Israeli victories, followed by the invasion of Lebanon and the massacres, created a new image in many minds, of an aggressive, expansionist state. In Israel too, the massacres and the bogged-down invasion were criticized in mass protest demonstrations. A Peace Now movement had been active in Israel since the late 1970s, but in crises the Israelis had always shown a united front. The Lebanon episode revealed for the first time a deep split between tough 'hawks' and more peace-inclined 'doves'.

After the 1982 massacres, divisions in Israel between warlike 'hawks' and peace-inclined 'doves' became deeper. Here, police stop a 1992 march by Israelis calling for the formation of separate Israeli and Palestinian states.

Israel withdrew from Lebanon in 1985, but maintained a 'security zone' in the south, run by its Maronite allies. The PLO never recovered its former strength in the area, but some PLO fighters did manage to return, and a separate guerrilla organization, Hizbollah, also kept up the struggle. Clearly Israel had not completely solved its Lebanon problem. But the next challenge would come even closer to home.

NEW STRATEGIES AND NEW CONFLICTS

After 1967, the main threat to Israel's security came from Arab states and the terrorist or guerrilla groups of the PLO, launching their attacks from Jordan or Lebanon. The Israeli-occupied territories remained quiet, except for a brief period in the early 1970s. They were largely left to manage their own affairs, and opportunities for work in Israel led to some economic progress. Local elections in 1976 showed that Palestinians in the Occupied Territories did support the PLO and resent Israeli rule, but violence was rare.

The situation began to change in the late 1970s, when Menachem Begin's government encouraged a rapid expansion of Jewish settlement in the Occupied Territories. A new generation of settlers moved into heavily populated areas, despite the hostility of their Palestinian neighbours. The settlers tended to be religiously motivated, arguing from their interpretation

West Bank Palestinians protest in 1989 against the spread of Jewish settlements into previously Arab-inhabited areas.

of the Bible that all of Palestine belonged to the Jews. Often the land they occupied had been confiscated from Arab owners, usually for 'security' reasons that seemed increasingly unconvincing.

The settlers remained a minority, but the impression grew that Israel intended gradually to absorb the Occupied Territories. This view was strengthened by Israeli maps issued from 1977, which no longer showed the country's 1949 borders. The implication was that the Occupied Territories had become a permanent part of Israel.

By the mid-1980s demonstrations and police actions had become common on the West Bank and the Gaza Strip. Israel was still troubled by attacks from outside, but struggles within the PLO limited its effectiveness, and the Arab states were distracted by problems such as the long and savage war waged between Iraq and Iran (1980-8).

The intifada

Although there was little prospect of outside help, the Arabs in the Occupied Territories mounted a spontaneous popular revolt, the intifada or uprising, which began in December 1987.

The intifada, 1988: stone-throwing Palestinian youths harass Israeli soldiers. This proved to be an effective, demoralizing tactic.

If the intifada had been an outright rebellion, conducted with guns, the Israeli army could have defeated it fairly easily. Instead, it involved protests, strikes and acts of non-cooperation such as non-payment of taxes and refusal to use identity documents. Israeli patrols were harassed by groups of youths and even children, whose stone-throwing injured and angered the soldiers but gave them no justification for shooting their tormentors – although, inevitably, some did open fire. In time the army developed anti-riot techniques, imposed curfews on the territories and even sealed them off from Israel. But arrests, beatings and the demolition of suspects' houses failed to end the intifada.

In the first three years, over a thousand Arabs were killed in the Occupied Territories. The brutality was not all on one side, for about a third of those who died were murdered by fellow-Arabs who suspected them of collaborating with the Israelis.

From armed struggle to civil disobedience

Hanan Ashrawi, a Palestinian woman professor, took part in the intifada and later became a leading peace negotiator. To her:

'The Palestinian intifada transformed ... Palestinian resistance from armed struggle to popular, and largely civil, disobedience. The focus shifted from a leadership in exile to a people under occupation, and rebellion began to take on the shape of nation building.'
(*This Side of Peace*)

Hanan Ashrawi campaigning in Palestinian national council elections at Ramallah on the West Bank, 1996.

No more violence?

After the first year of the intifada the PLO moved in and became its directing force. The power struggles within the organization were over and Yasser Arafat remained in command. But the destruction of Israel seemed as remote as ever, and late in 1988 Arafat announced a dramatic shift in policy. The PLO recognized Israel's right to exist in security and renounced all forms of terrorism. From now on the PLO would try to achieve its aims through political and diplomatic means.

Could he be trusted?

Even when the Palestinian leader, Yasser Arafat, renounced terrorism, groups inside the PLO went on with it. Was Arafat unable to control them, or was he insincere? Perhaps a bit of both. The British writer Michael Palumbo is very sympathetic towards the Palestinians. But he admits:

'Arafat had an ambivalent attitude towards the subject, at times seeming to tolerate or even encourage terrorism and at other times claiming to discourage it or even threatening to execute the perpetrators. While realizing its dangers, Arafat believed it was a useful negotiating card. He is quoted as saying: "As long as the world saw the Palestinians as no more than a people standing in line for UN rations, it was not likely to respect them. Now that they carry rifles, the situation has changed."'
(*Imperial Israel*)

The change was helped by the intifada, which showed that the Palestinians existed as a people and wanted to decide their own future. And ending terrorism meant that the USA was likely to take a more sympathetic attitude towards the PLO and the Palestinians. All the same, the new policy was a gamble for Arafat, and was not supported by all Palestinians.

In Israel, Begin had been succeeded as prime minister by the equally hard-line Yitzhak Shamir, who refused to be convinced that the PLO had changed in any essential respect. Shamir declared that Israel would not talk with terrorists, and he would not admit that the majority of Palestinians under Israeli rule supported the PLO.

Unyielding: Yitzhak Shamir, prime minister of Israel in 1983-4 and 1986-92.

By contrast, the USA accepted Arafat's statements and made its first official contacts with the PLO. However, difficulties arose in May 1990, when commandos of the Palestine Liberation Front (PLF) tried to land in Israel to attack a military camp. The PLF was one of the groups belonging to the PLO, but Arafat refused to act against the PLF or even condemn the failed attack; and as a result the USA broke off its talks with the PLO.

The incident showed how difficult it would be to make peace, even when both Arabs and Israelis were ready. Hard-liners would turn to violence to disrupt the peacemaking, and leaders on both sides would find it difficult to deal severely with their own people while taking a 'soft' line with the enemy.

The Iraqi dictator Saddam Hussein in 1991.

The Gulf crisis

Further complications were caused by the Gulf crisis of 1990-1. In a sudden strike, the Iraqi army occupied the small neighbouring state of Kuwait. The United Nations condemned the invasion and a huge military force was assembled by the USA and other powers, including several Arab states, ready to drive out the Iraqis if they refused to leave Kuwait.

The Iraqi dictator, Saddam Hussein, tried all sorts of tactics to divide or weaken the coalition that had been assembled against him. Attempting to win over the Arab peoples, he stated that Iraq would leave Kuwait if Israel withdrew from the Occupied Territories. The USA and its allies rejected this attempt to link two separate issues, but there was strong popular support for Iraq among the Palestinians, and Arafat and the PLO came out publicly on Saddam's side.

When the allies bombarded Iraq, Saddam's responses included damaging SCUD missile attacks on Israel. But Israel, normally quick to retaliate, was persuaded by the USA to stay out of the conflict. This made it

easier for Egypt and Syria to take part in a war on Iraq. The Gulf crisis ended with the liberation of Kuwait and the military defeat of Iraq, which was forced to make peace on the allies' terms.

Tel Aviv, 1991: the aftermath of an Iraqi SCUD missile attack on the city.

The outcome was a disaster for the PLO. Arafat's organization had angered the Americans. Worse, it had lost the vital financial support of Saudi Arabia and other oil-rich Arab states which had felt themselves threatened by Iraq. The PLO found itself in a weak position just when serious talks became possible.

Peacemaking

Having triumphed in the Gulf War, the Americans were now eager to settle outstanding world problems. Their influence was greater than ever because the Cold War was over and their former enemy, the Soviet Union, was on the verge of collapse.

The first step in US-sponsored peacemaking was a conference held in October 1991 at Madrid, the capital of Spain. The conference was attended by Israel, the Palestinians and Jordan. The PLO was not invited, since Israel would still have nothing to do with what it regarded as a terrorist organization, although it soon became obvious that the Palestinians at the conference were in fact PLO supporters. The PLO's willingness to reach agreement led to a quarrel with Hamas, a rival organization that was gaining some influence among the Palestinians.

Hard-liners, 1991: masked activists of the fundamentalist Hamas group walk through a Palestinian village.

Muslim fundamentalists at a religious rally wave Qur'ans and photos of Palestinian fighters.

The fundamentalists

Hamas, and the similar Islamic Jihad and Hizbollah movements, were inspired by religious ideals of a type that is usually described as fundamentalist – that is, they claimed to represent the true version of their religion, uncorrupted by modern ideas or interpretations. The fundamentalism of Hamas was matched by the kind of Jewish fundamentalism that was emerging in Israel, most aggressively among the settlers.

Both Muslim and Jewish fundamentalists aimed to create a state based on religious laws in which people with other beliefs would have no real voice. And both opposed any kind of

No compromise

Arab-Jewish conflicts lasted so long that many people on both sides yearned for peace. But extreme views also won support. The Gush Emunim movement, founded in 1974, has constantly urged Jewish settlement of the West Bank. It proclaimed that:

'the whole land of Israel [i.e. including the Occupied Territories] is the exclusive property of the Jewish people'.

The Muslim fundamentalist movement, Hamas, took an equally uncompromising view: the entire land must become an Islamic republic. One Hamas leader, Sheikh Jarror, declared:

'My goal is to educate people to reject the influence of Satan. I mean Israel.' (Quoted in Palumbo, *Imperial Israel*)

Armed, and not only with faith: a Jewish West Bank settler at prayer during a 1995 protest against the Palestinian-Israeli peace agreement and the planned transfer of territory to Palestinian control.

compromise peace which involved the sharing of Palestine between Arabs and Jews. If such a peace was ever made, the fundamentalists were certain to do all they could to destroy it.

In the early 1990s peace still seemed unlikely. There were more rounds of talks, but little progress was made. Then in June 1992 the Israelis elected a Labour government led by Yitzhak Rabin. Labour had always been more inclined to seek peaceful solutions than Likud, but almost at once terrorist attacks multiplied and street fighting broke out in the Gaza Strip. After more killings and kidnappings by Hamas, Rabin ordered the arrest of 1200 suspects, 413 of whom were deported to Lebanon.

Ironically, the rise of Hamas made some Israelis less hostile towards the PLO, which now seemed a moderate force. In January 1993 the ban on official Israeli contacts with the PLO was lifted at last. Yet at first there was still more violence, with killings and strikes and often vicious reprisals within Israel and the Occupied Territories, while Hizbollah launched rocket attacks from Lebanon.

At this bleak moment, without any warning, the world learned that peace had been made.

Tel Aviv, 1993: supporters of the Israeli Peace Now movement demonstrate in favour of the Oslo agreements between Israel and the Palestinians.

A beautiful nation?

During the intifada the journalist Janine di Giovanni visited the West Bank city of Jenin. She had a conversation with the uncle of a dead guerrilla, who said:

"'We are the Jews' cousins. From the same family tree. We don't hate the Jews for their religion. We lived together in the past and we can live together in the future."
"But," I said, "there was a time when the PLO said they wanted to throw all the Jews into the sea."
There was a brief scuffle of feet. The uncle cleared his throat.
"In Fatah we no longer say that we want to throw the Jews into the sea. When I dream of Palestine now, I dream of two nations living together, a peaceful nation. A beautiful nation.'" (*Against the Stranger: lives in occupied territory*)

A CHANCE FOR PEACE?

The August 1993 agreement between Israel and the PLO was not reached during the official talks in the US capital, Washington, DC. These talks were still going on when success was achieved in separate, completely secret negotiations that had been taking place in Norway for several months.

In the 'Oslo Accords', the PLO recognized Israel, renounced terrorism and accepted responsibility for the actions of all groups within the PLO. Israel recognized the PLO as the representative of the Palestinian people, and the two sides agreed upon plans for Palestinian self-rule and Israeli troop withdrawals. These were at first limited to the Gaza Strip and the West Bank city of Jericho, but it was expected that wider self-rule would follow in time, as Palestinians and Israelis learned to trust each other and work together. The most difficult issues – an independent Palestinian state, Jewish settlement on the West Bank and the future of East Jerusalem – were left for future discussion.

South Lebanon, 1993: Palestinian women and children at a refugee camp flourish portraits of Yasser Arafat and celebrate the Oslo Accords.

The Accords had many critics. Jewish settlers and fundamentalists were outraged by them. Likud opposed the agreement in the Knesset debate, but it was passed by 61 votes to 50. On the Palestinian side, Hamas and other fundamentalist groups remained violently hostile, and even some of Arafat's supporters felt that he had given Israel everything it wanted without getting very much in return. However, the agreement was received with enthusiasm in the wider world, and 43 nations pledged a $2,000,000,000 fund for development projects in the Occupied Territories.

Rabin, soldier-peacemaker

Yitzhak Rabin (1922-95) was an unlikely martyr for peace. Born in Jerusalem, he served with Jewish forces during the Second World War and was the Israeli army's Chief of Staff during the 1967 war. Later he became ambassador to the USA and prime minister (1974-7). As defence minister (1984-90) he had to deal with the intifada, and was widely believed to have told the soldiers 'Break their bones!' Rabin denied ever saying it, but he did tell the Knesset that the rising would be met with 'might, power and beatings'. Yet the strength of the intifada convinced him that Israel must make peace, and he won the 1992 elections, declaring:

'I am not ready to give up an inch of security, but I am ready to give up many inches of territory.'
(Quoted in Horovitz, ed., *Yitzhak Rabin: Soldier of Peace*)

Rabin the military man (right) with his former chief, General Moshe Dayan, who directed the 1967 campaign.

The first stages of the Oslo Accords went into effect in May 1994, when a new Palestinian police force took over the Gaza Strip and Jericho. Yasser Arafat returned from exile as head of the newly formed Palestinian Authority, and Israeli troops withdrew from most of the Gaza Strip. The Palestinian Authority soon

Against the Accords

Former Likud leader and prime minister Yitzhak Shamir (1915-) condemned the agreements between Israel and the PLO, writing in his autobiography that they were:

'negotiated ... hurriedly and recklessly entered into with the PLO by Israel's Labour Government ... these developments bear within them the seeds of disaster for the Jewish state.' (*Summing Up*)

acquired wider powers, and in September 1995 a new agreement ('Oslo II') visualized Israeli troop withdrawals from large areas of the West Bank in 1998.

Violence renewed

Even these limited advances were achieved in the face of great difficulties. As early as February 1994, a Jewish settler fired on praying Muslims, killing 29 before one of them managed to kill him. Many Israelis were killed or wounded as a result of kidnappings and suicide bombings, mainly by Hamas members. The new Palestinian police fired on Hamas demonstrators and arrested many militants. But in spite of it all, the peace held. Israel made peace with Jordan, and even Syria, one of Israel's most implacable enemies, proved willing to negotiate.

Rabin the peacemaker (left) shakes hands with Yasser Arafat after signing the 1993 peace agreement at Washington, DC. US president Bill Clinton looks on.

Then, on 4 November 1995, Yitzhak Rabin was assassinated. Ultra-nationalist groups had often chanted 'Traitor! Traitor!' when the names of Rabin or Peres were mentioned at a meeting, but few people had believed that any member of such groups would murder a fellow-Jew. The incident revealed just how dangerously divided Israel had become.

For a time, though, it seemed that the peace process would not be affected. Rabin was replaced as prime minister by Shimon Peres, who had led the peace negotiations with the PLO. An Israeli general election had to be held soon, but Labour seemed certain to win, since Likud, led by Binyamin Netanyahu, was widely blamed for violent anti-Rabin speeches which were felt to have encouraged his killer.

A dream of peace

Shimon Peres (1923-) held many high positions in Israel. Though a tough Labour politician, he was also a 'peacenik', willing to take part in secret meetings with Arab leaders. As foreign minister he negotiated the 1993 agreements with the PLO, and seemed to have crowned his career when he published his memoirs, claiming:

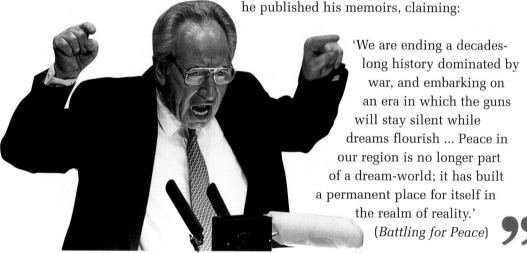

'We are ending a decades-long history dominated by war, and embarking on an era in which the guns will stay silent while dreams flourish ... Peace in our region is no longer part of a dream-world; it has built a permanent place for itself in the realm of reality.'
(*Battling for Peace*)

Dream in danger: Shimon Peres, no longer prime minister, attacks the policy of his successor, Binyamin Netanyahu, as a threat to peace.

An election upset

In the months before the election, many Israelis had second thoughts. A series of Hamas suicide bombings and Hizbollah attacks probably made many Israelis feel that it was not safe to give up any more land. Peres' commitment to peace was believed to be even stronger than Rabin's, and Likud ran a skilful election campaign portraying a Peres victory as a victory for weakness and renewed terrorism. At the end of May 1996, when the votes had been counted, Netanyahu had won by a narrow majority. Israel was to be led by a man who had opposed almost every aspect of the peace process.

Netanyahu takes power

Binyamin Netanyahu (1949-) took over as leader of the Likud party after its election defeat in 1991. His opposition to the Oslo peace process was based on distrust of the PLO, fears for Israel's security and an unwillingness to give up any Israeli-controlled territory.

On television and radio, in the run-up to the elections of 1996, Netanyahu told Israeli voters that the Rabin-Peres policy would mean that:

'a Palestinian state, with Jerusalem as its capital, will be set up; that we will get off the Golan Heights; and that we will face another, certain escalation of terror'.

The Palestinian Arabs were promised only that they would be able to:

'run just about every aspect of their daily lives with the exception of security and foreign affairs'. (Quoted in *Keesing's Record of World Events*, May 1996)

Binyamin Netanyahu.

Netanyahu claimed that he too wanted peace, but he rejected the possibility of a Palestinian state, refused even to consider returning the Golan Heights to Syria, and announced that he wanted to re-negotiate the September 1995 agreement. Perhaps more important were a series of government measures that seemed to have been designed to anger the Palestinians.

Proposals to build bridges to the Golan Heights and roads through the West Bank suggested that the Israeli occupation was to be permanent. A tunnel was opened under a holy place, the Temple Mount in Jerusalem, setting off Muslim riots. And after four years when there had been no new Jewish settlements on the West Bank or the Gaza Strip, confiscations of property began again, and government incentives encouraged the establishment of new Jewish communities.

Opposite: a focus of troubles to come? New buildings go up on the West Bank, earmarked for Jewish settlers.

The building of new housing at Har Homa, in East Jerusalem, was seen as another aggressive move, part of a plan to create a Jewish majority in the area.

After new suicide bombings, Netanyahu criticized Arafat's inability to prevent them, and declared that terrorism was the only subject on which Israel would negotiate. Then it became clear that he was planning to hand over less territory in 1998 than had been agreed at Oslo. By early 1998, US and EU efforts to keep the peace process going seemed to have failed. To complicate things even more, Netanyahu was finding it hard to hold his government together. The situation remained difficult and unpredictable.

 ### Threats of violence

By 1997 the peace process seemed to have stalled. The continued spread of Jewish settlement was said to have led to increased support for the Islamic militant group, Hamas. Hamas members carried out suicide missions, entering cafés and other public places with explosives strapped to their bodies. They detonated the explosives, killing themselves and others. One of their leaflets threatened that there was worse to come:

'Our next strikes will be cruel ...
We suggest to the Zionists that they open their hospitals and medical centres again to absorb more newcomers who will be shocked by our attacks. They will suffer from the fire of our holy war, which will burn every Jew in the land of Palestine.'
(Quoted in *The Guardian*, 6 August 1997)

DATE LIST

1896	First international congress of Zionists.
1914-18	The First World War.
1917, November	Balfour Declaration favours Jewish National Home.
1920, 1929, 1936-9	Violence in Palestine between Arabs, Jews and British security forces.
1937	Peel Commission recommends partition of Palestine.
1939	British authorities limit Jewish immigration into Palestine.
1939-45	The Second World War; Nazi Holocaust.
1947	British hand over Palestine problem to UN; majority of member states back partition.
1948	British leave Palestine. State of Israel proclaimed. First Arab-Israeli War.
1952	Egypt becomes a republic, led from 1954 by Nasser.
1956	Nasser nationalizes the Suez Canal. Second Arab-Israeli War and Anglo-French attack on Egypt.
1967, June	Six-Day War (third Arab-Israeli War). Defeated Arabs reject compromise at the Khartoum Conference.
1968	Israelis driven back at Karameh in Jordan. Arafat becomes leader of the PLO (Palestine Liberation Organization).
1973	Yom Kippur or October War (fourth Arab-Israeli War).
1974	PLO recognized by Arab states as 'sole legitimate representative' of the Palestinian people.
1977	Likud party takes power in Israel for first time. Sadat makes historic visit to Israel.
1979	Peace treaty signed between Israel and Egypt.
1980-88	Iran-Iraq War.
1981	Assassination of Sadat.
1982	Israel invades Lebanon. Falangists massacre Palestinians at Sabra and Chatila.
1985	Israel withdraws from Lebanon.
1987	Beginning of the intifada (Palestinian uprising against Israel).

1990-91	The Gulf crisis: Israel attacked by Iraqi missiles, but does not respond.
1991	Madrid peace conference.
1992	Yitzhak Rabin leads new Israeli government.
1993	Ban lifted on official Israeli contacts with PLO.
1993, August	Oslo Accords between Israel and the PLO.

1994	First stages of the Oslo Accords go into effect.
1995	'Oslo II' lays plans for further Israeli troop withdrawals.
1995	Assassination of Rabin.
1996	Likud leader Binyamin Netanyahu becomes Israeli prime minister.
1997	The peace process stalls.

RESOURCES

RECOMMENDED READING

Heather Bleaney and Richard Lawless, *The Arab-Israeli Conflict 1947-67*, Batsford, 1990: a series of short biographies of people involved in the conflict.

Martin Gilbert, *The Arab-Israeli Conflict: Its History in Maps*, Weidenfeld, 1992 edition: this makes an interesting and different way to follow a complicated history.

The following are more traditional in approach. They are all short and try to be fair, so it is worth reading them and comparing their differences of emphasis and sympathies:

Paul Harper, *The Arab-Israeli Conflict*, Wayland, 1989

John King, *The Gulf War*, Wayland, 1991

John King, *Conflict in the Middle East*, Wayland, 1993

Stewart Ross, *The Arab-Israeli Conflict*, Evans, 1995

FICTION AND FILM

English-language novels and films tend to concentrate on Jewish experiences and the impact of terrorism. Even the best are one-sided, but a few make some attempt to understand the point of view of the Palestinians or terrorist groups. Two good thrillers about terrorism are: Eric Ambler, *The Levanter*, Weidenfeld, 1972; and John Le Carré, *The Little Drummer Girl*, Hodder, 1983.

The persecutions of European Jews and the Nazi Holocaust have been widely treated in books and films. *The Diary of Anne Frank* is easy for a young person to relate to. Thomas Keneally's book *Schindler's Ark* (1982) and the film version, *Schindler's List* (1993), are currently well-known and widely available; they focus on the efforts of a German businessman during the Second world War to save the Jewish workers in his factory.

The best-known Israeli movie, *Hill 24 Doesn't Answer* (1955), follows the experiences of four soldiers defending a hill outside Jerusalem. You are more likely to come across such pro-Israeli American films as *Exodus* (1960), *Cast a Giant Shadow* (1966), *Victory at Entebbe* (1976) and *Operation Thunderbolt* (1977). *The Little Drummer Girl* (1984) is a filmed version of Le Carré's novel.

GLOSSARY

Ashkenazim   Jews from Eastern Europe.

Cold War   extreme hostility (but without fighting) between alliances led by the USA and the Soviet Union.

Diaspora   dispersion of the Jews beyond Palestine.

dumdum bullet   deadly type of bullet which expands on impact.

Falangist   member of a Lebanese Christian militia or political party.

Fatah   organization led by Yasser Arafat; it became part of the PLO.

fedayeen   Palestinian Arab guerrillas or terrorists who launched cross-border attacks on Israel.

fundamentalist   person who believes in a traditional, usually severe or militant, version of religion.

Gaza Strip   Arab-inhabited coastal area conquered by Israel in 1967.

Gush Emunim   militant Jewish Israeli group; fundamentalist.

Haganah   Jewish military force, basis of the later Israeli army.

Hamas   militant Palestinian Muslim group; fundamentalist.

Hizbollah   militant anti-Israel Muslim group based in Lebanon.

Holy Land   another name for Palestine.

intifada   Palestinian uprising against Israel from December 1987.

Irgun Zvai Leumi   Jewish guerrilla or terrorist group.

Islamic Jihad   anti-Israel Muslim group; fundamentalist.

kibbutz   idealistic Jewish farming co-operative (plural kibbutzim).

Knesset   Israel's parliament.

League of Nations   Assembly bringing together representatives of all states; succeeded in 1945 by the UN.

Likud   group of Israeli political parties; main opponent of Labour Party.

mandated territory   territory entrusted to a great power by the League of Nations.

Maronite   Lebanese Christian.

nakhbeh   Arabic, 'catastrophe': Palestinian term for the 1948-9 war.

Occupied Territories   territory conquered by Israel in the 1967 war.

PFLP   Popular Front for the Liberation of Palestine: anti-Israel guerrilla or terrorist group, mainly based in Syria.

PLO   Palestine Liberation Organization: main organization representing Palestinian Arabs.

Sephardic Jew   Jew of Arab, North African or Spanish origin.

Shia   important Muslim sect, but less numerous than Sunnis.

Sunni   Muslim sect; the great majority of Muslims are Sunnis.

West Bank   area west of the river Jordan, conquered by Israel in 1967.

Zionism   movement to found a Jewish state in Palestine.

INDEX

SOURCES

The quotations in this book were taken from: Hanan Ashrawi, *This Side of Peace: a personal account*, Simon and Schuster, 1995; David Ben-Gurion, *Israel: Years of Challenge*, Anthony Blond, 1963; Moshe Dayan, *The Story of My Life*, Sphere, 1976; Jonathan Dimbleby, *The Palestinians*, Quartet Books, 1980; Janine di Giovanni, *Against the Stranger: lives in occupied territory*, Viking, 1993; Theodor Herzl, *The Jewish State*, 1896; David Horovitz, ed., *Yitzhak Rabin: Soldier of Peace* by the staff of *The Jerusalem Report*, Peter Halban Publishers, 1996; Josephus, *The Jewish War*, Penguin Classics, 1981; *Keesing's Record of World Events*, May 1996;

Henry Kissinger, *Years of Upheaval*, Weidenfeld, 1982; Walter Laqueur, *The Arab-Israeli Reader*, Weidenfeld, 1968; Conor Cruise O'Brien, *The Siege: the saga of Israel and Zionism*, Weidenfeld, 1986; Michael Palumbo, *Imperial Israel: the history of the occupation of the West Bank and Gaza*, Bloomsbury, 1990; Shimon Peres, *Battling for Peace*, Weidenfeld, 1995; Stewart Ross, *The Arab-Israeli Conflict*, Evans, 1995; Rinna Samuel, *A History of Israel*, Weidenfeld, 1989; Yitzhak Shamir, *Summing Up: an autobiography*, Weidenfeld, 1994; John and Janet Wallach, *Arafat: in the eyes of the beholder*, Heinemann, 1991.